The Questioner's Prayer

To Msgr. Robert Treviso

Fraternally,

+ Robt. J. Baker
Bishop of Charleston

The Questioner's Prayer

Bishop Robert J. Baker

Our Sunday Visitor Publishing Division
Our Sunday Visitor, Inc.
Huntington, Indiana 46750

Nihil Obstat:
Rev. Michael Heintz
Censor Librorum

Imprimatur:
✠ John M. D'Arcy
Bishop of Fort Wayne-South Bend
December 22, 2006

The *Nihil Obstat* and *Imprimatur* are official declarations that a book or pamphlet is free of doctrinal or moral error. No implication is contained therein that those who have granted the *Nihil Obstat* or *Imprimatur* agree with the contents, opinions, or statements expressed.

Our Sunday Visitor Publishing Division
Our Sunday Visitor, Inc.
200 Noll Plaza
Huntington, IN 46750

ISBN: 978-1-59276-238-5 (Inventory No. T289)
LCCN: 2007921686

Cover design by Amanda Miller
Artwork by Christopher J. Pelicano
Interior design by Sherri L. Hoffman

PRINTED IN THE UNITED STATES OF AMERICA

DEDICATED TO

My brother, Jim Baker, and my sister-in-law, Arlene Baker, both of whom faced the question "Why Lord?" while struggling with cancer and turned to God often in prayer, finding consolation and strength in their faith.

The ultimate question is always a question about God,
it is always a question about the meaning of life,
about the beginning and especially about
the end of the road that we traverse on earth.

— POPE JOHN PAUL II

In a place where words fail;
in the end there can only be dread silence —
a silence which is itself a heartfelt cry to God:
Why, Lord, did you remain silent?
How could you tolerate all this?

— POPE BENEDICT XVI AT AUSCHWITZ-BRIKENAU, MAY 2006

Contents

Preface

Often when people enter a Church to prepare for Holy Mass, or try to rivet their attention on the particular service they are attending, they get distracted by the thousand and one preoccupations of everyday life. Some of those distractions are about the problems they are facing that day. Some go much deeper — to the questions they have buried within them that never quite come to the surface, questions that deal with serious issues they are facing in their relationship with God.

My intention in this book is to help people bring those questions to God in prayer and to remind them how the questioner's prayer, with a little help from God and the intercession of the Blessed Mother, can become a prayer of faith.

Times When We Question

Following a great tragedy or disaster, human or natural, we may be led to ask questions of God. *God, where were you in the midst of all this?* Like Martha, confronting Jesus after the death of her brother, Lazarus, we may be led to suggest that the tragedy would not have happened, if only "you had been here," forgetting that a fundamental teaching of our faith is that God is always present.

At the outset, then, it is important to point out that not all questioners' prayers arise from faith or lead to faith. Some arise from despair; and one can only hope that at some future point, they will evolve into a prayer of faith and abandonment to God, in the way Jesus ultimately commended Himself to the Father on the cross.

In the Scriptures we find that Zechariah's questioning attitude in the face of the great revelation by the Archangel Gabriel that his wife, Elizabeth, was to bear a son, reflected disbelief on his part (". . . you did not believe my words," Lk. 1:20). Because of this, he lost the ability to speak until the fulfillment of the miraculous birth of his son, John the Baptist. The age factor prompted Zechariah's initial disbelief.

Even Moses and Aaron were denied access to the Promised Land "because both of you broke faith with me among the Israelites at the waters of Meribath-kadesh in the wilderness of Zin, by failing to maintain my holiness among the Israelites" (Deut. 32:51). Moses was told he could view the land at a distance only, but not enter into it (Deut. 32:52).

Turning to God in a time of quandary and distress is itself a great act of faith. While we struggle to understand His will, we nonetheless cry out to Him with our questions. May the Lord bless those who bring these sincere questions to Him. If you are one of those people, you stand in a long line of biblical giants like the Psalmist, Job, St. Peter, and the other apostles, who had many questions for their God. These questions came from a perspective of faith that the God whom they questioned would answer in due time.

In writing this book it is my intention to help you give voice to the questions you have for God in prayer — from a perspective of faith.

MOST REVEREND ROBERT J. BAKER
September 14, 2006
The Exaltation of the Holy Cross

A cursory glance at ancient history shows clearly how in different parts of the world, with their different cultures, there arise at the same time the fundamental questions which pervade human life: Who am I? Where have I come from and where am I going? Why is there evil? What is there after this life? We find these questions in the sacred writings of Israel, as also in the Veda and the Avesta; we find them in the writings of Confucius and Lao-Tze, and in the preaching of Tirthankara and Buddha; they appear in the poetry of Homer and in the tragedies of Euripides and Sophocles, as they do in the philosophical writings of Plato and Aristotle. They are questions which have their common source in the quest for meaning which has always compelled the human heart. In fact, the answer given to these questions decides the direction which people seek to give to their lives.

— POPE JOHN PAUL II, *FIDES ET RATIO* (ENCYCLICAL ON FAITH AND REASON)

Introduction

Questions

Flying on a plane can be an interesting venture, especially if you are wearing a Roman collar and praying your Breviary (i.e., Liturgy of the Hours). On a recent flight a fellow passenger, sitting one seat ahead of me across the aisle, handed me a folded piece of paper, which I originally thought he had mistakenly picked up off the floor to return to me. He motioned for me to open it. Inside was a plea for me to help him through a crisis. His wife had taken up with another man and was living in adultery. Did I have a Scripture passage for him to read to help him through this difficult situation?

By "coincidence," I did. It was the psalm that I was reading at the time and seemed perfect for the occasion. I wrote the passage down on the piece of paper he had given me and gave him my address and phone number. Later on, in the airport, I had the chance to speak with him briefly.

> *But I call upon God,*
> *and the LORD will save me.*
> *Evening and morning and at noon*
> *I utter my complaint and moan,*
> *and he will hear my voice.*
> *He will redeem me unharmed*
> *from the battle that I wage,*
> *for many are arrayed against me.*
>
> Ps. 55:16-18

On another flight, a man in his twenties was sitting next to me and thought he recognized me from somewhere. He did. I had been pastor for thirteen years in a city where he grew up. His mother was Catholic, but not his father. He had never been baptized, but his grandmother had been working on his conversion for years.

Tragedy had struck his family. His father had taken his own life some time before, and that had left a heavy burden on his family. He had question after question after question on my perspectives on life in general. His life was incomplete. He seemed ready to look into the Catholic faith. I gave him a name of a priest he might contact and explained to him how he might become a follower of Christ in the Catholic Church . . . all on a plane flight from Dallas to Atlanta.

Both of these men were facing difficult situations that brought them to the point of asking serious questions about life in general and faith in particular. It was the trying situations of life that brought them not to despair, but to faith — at least the minimal amount of faith needed to begin a serious quest. Isn't that what faith is all about? It is the starting point for our encounter with God, and often, it begins with a question.

There may be a question in our hearts that we haven't quite answered yet, one that we really need to answer before we can move ahead in faith, hope, and love. It may be a question we want to direct to God in prayer:

Why, God?

How, God?

When, God?

What, God?

Where, God?

Who, God?

Ask the question and you are on the way to a good prayer, a solid encounter with the living God, who wants to meet you as you are — where you are.

The Gospel Way

Have you ever noticed how often people asked questions of Jesus in the Gospels? Here are few examples:

- Nicodemus, a Pharisee, in a clandestine conversation in the night, asks him, "How can a man be born after having grown old?" (Jn. 3:4).
- A man of means puts the question to Jesus, "Good Teacher, what must I do to inherit eternal life?" (Mk.10:17).
- Peter asks how often he should forgive when his brother wrongs him: "As many as seven times?" (Mt. 18:21).

Jesus did not back away from the questions people asked Him. He welcomed them. And in each situation, He gave an answer that guided the one posing that question.

The people in the Gospels who put questions to Jesus hold a special place in the Christian dispensation. They evoked a teaching from Him that gave direction not only to their lives, but to the lives of all who have picked up the Gospels in the centuries that followed.

The "questioners" were not afraid to acknowledge a little of their ignorance in their quest for meaning and purpose in life.

Jesus stood still and called them, saying, "What do you want me to do for you?"

— Mt. 20:32

Like the Psalmist before them, they sensed that God was not put off by questions. "I call upon you," the author of Ps. 17

cried out, "for you will answer me, O God; incline your ear to me; hear my words."

In Mark's and Luke's Gospels, we find one situation where the disciples backed away from questioning Jesus. This occurs when He discusses His impending suffering and death (Mk. 9:32; Lk. 9:45). We are told the disciples were simply "afraid to question him" about the matter.

Apart from this occasion they appear far from gun-shy in the Gospels. They wanted to know, and they weren't afraid to ask.

Seek and You Shall Find

People who ask questions learn. We often think the questioning person is the class "dummy," but in reality, the questioner is often the most intelligent one in any group; and if he isn't, he becomes so quickly. Simon Peter's seemingly ridiculous questions and comments resulted in some of Jesus' greatest lessons. For all his shortcomings, Peter was intelligent enough not to hide his ignorance. He revealed his lack of knowledge and faith by the questions he asked, and these questions resulted in a speedy revelation of the Lord's will for him.

Pope John Paul II talked about the quest for truth as being a source of inspiration in work and in science, but he said that the hunger for the truth in our souls goes even further.

> The ultimate question is always a question about God; it is always a question about the meaning of human life, about the beginning and especially about the end of the road that we traverse on earth. We must live by the truth; we must seek it; we must tend toward it. We cannot make any sense of or live by falsehood.

That is why the "Questioner's Prayer" is so important. The questioner is the one seeking the truth about life and about love.

The "Other" Type of Prayer

You may have heard in the past about the four kinds of prayer, summed up by the mnemonic "ACTS":

Adoration, in which we praise and adore God.

Contrition, in which we express sorrow for our sins to God.

Thanksgiving, in which we express our gratitude for all that God has done for us.

Supplication, in which we express our needs to God.

There is one other type of prayer — the prayer of interrogation, the "Questioner's Prayer." It, too, is real prayer. When we're confused or in a quandary, one of the sincerest prayers we can address to God is the prayer that expresses our confusion in a heartfelt manner: "How, God? When, God? What, God? Where, God? Who, God?"

Only if we ask questions can we expect answers, from God as well as one another. A question put to God can be a real sign of faith and trust in Him and the beginning of a profound loving relationship with Him for life, even when life may appear to be at its darkest hour.

I. Why?

Why, Lord?

"Eli, Eli, lema sabachthani?"
that is, "My God, my God,
why have you forsaken me?"
— MT. 27:46

The Prayer of Jesus

The greatest "why" prayer of all time was uttered by Jesus to His Father as He was dying, crucified on the cross.

The Son of God cried out to His Father, uttering the words of Ps. 22, verse 2, "My God, my God, why have you forsaken me?" *"Eli, Eli, lema sabachthani?"*

Jesus knew words from that psalm by heart. He must have prayed them many times:

> *My God, my God, why have you forsaken me?*
> *Why are you so far from helping me, from the words of my*
>   *groaning?*
> *O my God, I cry out by day, but you do not answer;*
> *and by night, but find no rest.*
>
> — PS. 22:2-3

It is a prayer of utter desolation, the kind of prayer one only utters when God seems far away. The Psalmist who first uttered that prayer spoke from the depths of his heart. It was an honest description of how he felt. And he, in faith, let God know how bad his situation was.

Jesus on the cross, in His humanity, must have felt so utterly alone. After all, He was abandoned by almost all of His followers.

In their cowardice they fled to higher ground for safety. The scourgings, the taunts, the jeers, the spitting in His face, the cruelty of the executioners, all added to the desolation He felt. God the Father allowed Jesus, in His Passion and death, to suffer the agony of loneliness, as any human being might suffer in the face of death.

Within each form of suffering endured by man, and at the same time at the basis of the whole world of suffering, there inevitably arises the question: Why?[1]

— POPE JOHN PAUL II

"My God, my God, why have you forsaken me?" This is the great prayer presented from the cross for our Good Friday meditations annually. Can we fathom the depth of pain Jesus suffered for us on the cross? Never. Mel Gibson tried to suggest that the Passion of Jesus was more than we could ever imagine, and he was right. But even his monumental effort falls short in translation. Jesus suffered so greatly for us that He prayed the "why" prayer to the Father.

At a Loss

Often, we encounter people trying to make sense out of tragedies suddenly thrust upon them out of the blue.

I met one such person in the Blessed Sacrament Chapel of a parish where I was preparing for the Sacrament of Confirmation. He was grieving over the breakup of his marriage and asking God why this was happening to him. Why was his wife taking up with another man, and why was he risking the loss of his daughter when he had worked so conscientiously to live his faith and practice it fervently?

In the aftermath of her son's tragic death, Tina Williams said, "We're asking God a lot, 'Why?'"[2]

Matthew Williams was trying to earn some money after high school graduation to buy a car and prepare for college. His father helped him get a job similar to his work as a pipefitter, and he worked with his father on board the USNS Supply, a government-owned supply ship undergoing repairs in North Charleston. He had been working on the consolidated holding tank (CHT) room, removing pipes from the tank along with two other men (his father was not with him that day); when they loosened one particular pipe, sewage began spilling out. All three fled the room, but then, Matthew went back to retrieve his hard hat and some tools.

He was found shortly thereafter, lying on his back in about three inches of liquid. An autopsy report indicated that Matthew had died as a result of toxic fumes caused by the presence of hydrogen sulfide, a colorless gas produced by raw sewage. Daniel and Tina, saddened by the loss of their dear son, were led to ask the question, "Why, Lord?"

A Pope Asks "Why?"

When Pope Benedict XVI visited the horrible site of the former Nazi death camps of Auschwitz-Birkenau in May of 2006, he uttered the "why" prayer. He noted that it was almost impossible even to speak in a place of where such horror had been experienced by human beings and that it was particularly difficult and troubling for a Christian and a pope from Germany. The pope asked from the depth of his soul:

In a place like this words fail; in the end there can only be a dread silence — a silence which is itself a heartfelt cry to God:

Why, Lord, did you remain silent?
How could you tolerate all this? [3]

Having visited those two death camps myself in the fall of 2005, with three rabbis and five other American bishops, I could easily identify with the sentiments Pope Benedict expressed in his questioner's prayer to God.

The Perpetual Question

After the devastating tsunami on December 26, 2004, a daily paper carried an article titled *When Disaster Strikes, People Ask: Why Does God Allow Suffering?* [4] The piece began with the observation that if God is all-powerful and all-good, "why does He permit suffering on the scale of the disaster that struck such a blow against South and Southeast Asia?"[5]

Theologians and journalists weighed in with their explanations of this terrible tragedy. Why would God allow such a terrible event to occur that would take the lives of thousands of people?

Those of us who live in the United States experienced a disaster of great magnitude on September 11, 2001, with the terrorists' attack that killed thousands at the World Trade Center in New York, the Pentagon in Washington, and on the downed plane in Pennsylvania. On that occasion, many people asked, "Why?"

Thus says the LORD:
A voice is heard in Ramah,
lamentation and bitter weeping.
Rachel is weeping for her children;
she refuses to be comforted
for her children,
because they are no more.

Thus says the LORD:
Keep your voice from weeping,
and your eyes from tears;
for there is a reward for your work,
says the LORD:
they shall come back from the
land of the enemy;
there is hope for your future,
says the LORD:
your children shall come back
to their own country.

— JER. 31:15-17

Even more recently, in 2005, the people of Mississippi and Louisiana experienced devastating losses due to Hurricane Katrina — a heavy toll in lives and massive loss of property.

In the face of our own personal struggles, failures, losses, serious illnesses, family or relational problems, financial setbacks, human weakness, and sinfulness, we, too, may come to the point of asking God, "Why?" "My God, my God, why have you forsaken me?"

Walking with Christ on the Way to Calvary

I suggest we can do no better than take that question to God in prayer and listen carefully for His answer. The prayer we might use in our meditation for this season, or any season of the year, could be the Way of the Cross.

My brother Jim, who faced a long bout with cancer prior to his death on December 31, 2006, wrote a powerful meditation on uniting his suffering with that of Christ in a preface to the book *Stations of the Cross for the Sick*[6], written by Kitty McDonough. Jim found a "real connection to the journey of Jesus" through His most difficult times. He could imagine Our Lord's anxiety and pain; at the same time, he was touched by Jesus' compassion for others on the way to Calvary, when He was the one who was suffering so. Jim was moved by Jesus' forgiveness of the people who led Him to Calvary and His love for them.

Often, we cannot understand why God refrains from intervening. Yet he does not prevent us from crying out, like Jesus on the Cross: "My God, my God, why have you forsaken me?" (Mt. 27:46). We should continue asking this question in prayerful dialogue before his face: "Lord, holy and true, how long will it be?" (Rev. 6:10).

— POPE BENEDICT XVI, *DEUS CARITAS EST*

Jim saw how Jesus kept His sight fixed on His mission, never quitting or giving in or complaining. He remained faithful to the end. A teacher all through His life, through His passion and death, Jesus taught His followers how to approach death.

After reading my brother's reflections, I could not imagine a better source of strength for all people who are ill or suffering than meditating on the Passion of Jesus Christ, especially with the help of meditations on the Way of the Cross of Jesus. As people unite their struggles with the Lord and His struggles, their crosses would become His and would be easier to bear.

A Living Example of the Way of the Cross

Pope John Paul II's public suffering prior to his death on the eve of Divine Mercy Sunday[7] gave witness to his profound spiritual understanding of the power of grace that comes with linking one's suffering with the suffering of Jesus Christ. The pope's lived experienced of suffering, and the tremendous witness he gave to the world as to how to bear suffering, is among one of his greatest gifts to the Church and to the world.

Even after taking two bullets from an assassin, and in the face of arthritis and Parkinson's disease, the pope still felt compelled to travel to various parts of the world. This had to cause even more suffering for him, but one always got the impression that he wouldn't let a little thing like pain slow him down. He was unstoppable, a man of great spiritual energy, even in the midst of serious illness.

Just a little over a year before his death, the pope granted Bishop Thompson (my predecessor) and me a twenty-minute private audience during our *ad limina* visit. It struck me that, as long as he humanly could, Pope John Paul was willing to give people like ourselves the time of day. He felt it was important to be of support to visiting bishops, even in his illness. The reason he could pull all that off when the rest of us would have hoisted the white flag of surrender was his ability to link his sufferings with the sufferings of the Lord.

I believe Pope John Paul gave an inside view of wherein lay his spiritual resources in his 1984 Apostolic Letter on the meaning of human suffering, *Salvifici Doloris*. There, he wrote:

> Christ does not explain in the abstract the reasons for suffering, but before all else he says: "Follow me! Come! Take part through your suffering in this work of saving the world, a salvation achieved through my suffering! Through my cross!" Gradually, as the individual takes up his cross, spiritually uniting himself to the cross of Christ, the salvific meaning of suffering is revealed before him. He does not discover this meaning at his own human level, but at the level of the suffering of Christ.[8]

These words from *Salvifici Doloris* were released to the world a few years after the assassination attempt in St. Peter's Square (May 13, 1981). The Pope had a lot of time to reflect on suffering as he lay recovering in a hospital, following a close call with death.

In addition to the physical recovery involved came emotional pain as well, when he visited his assailant, Ali Agca, in prison. The Pope's secretary, now Cardinal Stanislaw Dziwisz, said that he witnessed this visit in person. "The Pope had already publicly pardoned him in his very address after the attack," says the former secretary. "[But] I did not hear the prisoner utter a single word to ask for forgiveness." That, too, had to have been a great spiritual suffering for the pontiff.

In faith, he could easily have prayed the "Why, Lord?" prayer a time or two.

Abandonment to God's Will

Pope John Paul gained his resolve from his deep faith. As it was for the Psalmist and for Jesus, so also for ourselves, the "why" prayer can become transformed into a prayer of trust and resignation to God's holy will. The prayer in the Psalms that begins "My God, my God, why have you forsaken me?" ends with:

> *But you O LORD, do not be far away!*
> *O my help, come quickly to my aid!*
>
> *For he did not despise or abhor*
> *the affliction of the afflicted;*
> *he did not hide his face from me,*
> *but heard when I cried to him.*
>
> — Ps. 22:19, 24

As for Jesus, Luke's Gospel presents His final words as spoken from the cross around midday — after darkness had descended over the region until midafternoon:

> *Jesus, crying with a loud voice, said, "Father, into your hands*
> *I commend my spirit." Having said this, he breathed his last.*
>
> — Lk. 23:46

Our Response

When confronted with the prayer "Why, Lord?", we can choose any number of solutions, from seeking counsel from a wise priest to talking with a seasoned counselor or someone who has suffered as we have. But don't forget the one who said "I am the way." Meditations on His Way of the Cross can move us spiritually to link our quandary, our question, our heaviness of heart, and our suffering with that of Jesus — and if we are patient, He will most likely, in turn, put in our heart trust and resignation to God's holy will by making us realize how great is God's love for us.

PRAYER

Lord, hear my cry; listen to my question — "why?"
For it rises to You from the depth of my heart,
as a prayer from one
who truly believes in You,
but experiences You right now as far away from me.
O Lord,
Be not far from me.
Hasten to help me.
I need You to answer my plea.
Turn not Your face from me.
I seek to understand Your ways and to follow
Your holy will for me.
Help me to find strength for my journey
and light for my path as I join
my suffering to that of Your Son's suffering
and death on the cross.
May the Passion of Jesus give meaning
and hope to me as I experience
my own personal passion.
Into Your hands, O Lord, in faith and in trust,
I commend my spirit.
Amen.

Additional Resources

For additional reading on the subject of suffering, you may wish to consult Pope John Paul II's 1984 Apostolic Letter on Suffering, *Salvifici Doloris*, available in Catholic bookstores. Also valuable books on suffering are:

Father Benedict Groeschel, *Arise from Darkness: What to do When Life Doesn't Make Sense* (San Francisco, CA: Ignatius Press, 1995)

Peter Kreeft, *Making Sense Out of Suffering* (Cincinnati, OH: St. Anthony Press, 1986)

Patricia Livingston, *Let in the Light: Facing the Hard Stuff with Hope* (Notre Dame, IN: Sorin Books, 2006)

Father F. J. Remler, *Why Must I Suffer? A Book of Light and Consolation* (Fitzwilliam, NH: Loretto Press, 2003)

Michael Dubruiel, *The Power of the Cross: Applying the Passion of Christ to Your Life* (Huntington, IN: Our Sunday Visitor Publishing Division, 2004)

Catalina Ryan McDonough, *Stations of the Cross for the Sick* (Huntington, IN: Our Sunday Visitor Publishing Division, 2002)

Theresa Burke / Kevin Burke, *From Grief to Grace: Healing the Wounds of Abuse, Reclaiming the Gift of Sexuality* (Rachel's Vineyard Ministries [610-354-0555])

St. Pio / Patricia Treece, Editor, *Through the Year with Padre Pio: 365 Daily Readings* (Ann Arbor, MI: Charis Books, 2003)

II. How?

"How can this be?"
— Lk. 1:34

Amazement

The question "How can this be?" was addressed to the Archangel Gabriel by a young woman named Mary, from a town of Galilee called Nazareth, who was promised in marriage to a man named Joseph, a descendent of King David.

The Archangel Gabriel had just appeared to Mary and brought her the astounding news that she had been highly favored by God and, as a grace-filled woman, would give birth to the Son of the Most High God. Her Son would be king of the descendants of Jacob forever, and His kingdom would never end.

Mary was rightly surprised. As the most prudent Virgin, she asked, "How will this be done?"

In response, Gabriel explained God's plan for His people. Mary was to play a dramatic role, a vital role, in that plan. The Holy Spirit would bring about the conception of this child without the intervention of any human father.

Nothing is impossible with God.

In her profound and simple faith, Mary believed that. She had always held that belief; and what's more, she lived that belief. Now, that belief would be put to the test. Her question "How can this be?" was a question addressed out of faith in God, not out of resistance to or doubt of God's plan, or rejection of God's holy will for her.

What initial response would we expect from this simple woman of faith other than the question, "How is this possible, Lord?"

On the surface, Mary saw a lot of obstacles. First of all, she was a virgin. Second, in her humility she sought to know her part in this great task presented to her. Also, she most likely was thinking about Joseph, that kindly, holy man who had sought her hand in marriage. What about him? What would his reaction be? And her parents and family members, what would they think about her?

And the Son she would bear — what would motherhood of such a special Son mean for her? What would being His mother entail?

She knew there was a mystery being revealed to her, and she could never completely understand it. So she asked directions on what was God's will for her.

The Fourth Station of the Cross presents Jesus as meeting His mother on the way to Calvary. Motherhood, for Mary, was a commitment not just to conceiving a child and giving birth to that child, but rearing that child lovingly and identifying with all the joys and sorrows of that child through life. Maternity would mean suffering, at times great suffering. Mary was committing her life to all that her unique Son would do, and be, for the people of Israel and all of humanity.

How would all of this be possible? Mary had a seemingly insurmountable challenge before her.

Contrasting "Hows" of Zechariah and Mary

In contrast to the faithful acceptance of the "how" prayer of Mary when faced with a similar announcement from the Archangel Gabriel, Zechariah hesitated to put his full confidence in God's providential authority. He, too, was faced with a major dilemma: his wife was beyond the childbearing years and apparently unable to conceive a child. Zechariah's hesitancy to accept God's decree is indicated to us in Scripture as a lack of faith. His "how" prayer was not one of faith.

Mary's question, "How is this possible?", stemmed from her deep faith in God. She was not questioning God's ability to follow through with a promise, even under adverse conditions, as apparently Zechariah was. She was wondering about her own ability to accomplish the task and her personal worthiness to assume so important a responsibility. Mary never doubted God's faithfulness. She had complete confidence in God's ability to work in her life.

In her humility, she was asking how God would use a simple vessel like herself to accomplish so noble an end, given the fact that she knew not man (Lk. 1:34). Mary believed in God's faithfulness to His promises nonetheless. In a joyful response to the angel's annunciation, she sang God's praises, while Zechariah was left speechless until the Word had been fulfilled.

In one of his famous discourses, St. Bernard compares Mary to the star that navigators seek so as not lose their course: "Whoever you are who perceive yourself during this mortal existence to be drifting in treacherous waters at the mercy of winds and the waves rather than walking on firm ground, turn your eyes not away from the splendor of this guiding star, unless you wish to be submerged in the storm! . . .
Look at the star, call upon Mary . . . With her for a guide, you will never go astray; . . . under her protection, you have nothing to fear; if she walks with you, you will not grow weary; if she shows you favor you will reach the goal" (Hom. *Super Missus Est,* II, 17).

— POPE BENEDICT XVI, *ANGELUS,* AUGUST 20, 2006

A Necessary Question

Before any of us launches our own projects or plans, in pondering our own responsibilities in life, we, too, ask the question "how?" We would be foolish not to ask that question in carrying out our everyday duties. We know ourselves too well to suggest instant success. We know the many hazards that lie before us.

The apostles themselves repeatedly had to struggle with their own limitations and their failures to measure up to the task of being a faithful disciple of Jesus. When Peter attempted to suggest to Jesus another path than the suffering that lay ahead, the Lord rebuked him, called him "Satan" and an obstacle in his way. The Lord did this because Peter's thoughts came not from God but from human nature (Mt. 16:23). How often the apostles must have asked the Lord for forgiveness for their failures to allow him to help them believe, hope, and love!

So how can we weak, feeble human beings take on the great challenges facing us in life? How do we handle constructively all of the struggles facing us in life as well as all the good that God might send our way? Like:

- a wayward son or daughter
- an unexpected pregnancy
- an unfaithful spouse
- a hard-to-live-with parent entrusted to our care
- a boss never satisfied with our labor
- end-of-the-month bills and no money to pay them
- a sudden unforeseen, serious illness

Throughout our lives, we are presented with unexpected (and, in many cases, unwanted) situations; in all of these, we are apt to ask, "How, Lord?" How we ask God — either in faith like Mary, or doubt like Zechariah — will have the same predictable result: in one case, praise . . . in the other, mute silence.

I suggest, not surprisingly, that you and I look to Mary as our model when facing the unexpected that leads to us asking the question "How, Lord?" Mary heard the answer to her dilemma from the Archangel Gabriel: "Nothing is impossible with God." And her response was, "Here I am, the servant of the Lord; let it be with me according to your word" (Lk. 1:38). May God's holy will be done — *fiat!* If God wills it, I want that for my life, too.

In the first place, beg of God by most earnest prayer, that He perfect whatever good you begin, in order that He who has been pleased to count us in the number of His children, need never be grieved at our evil deeds.

— St. Benedict, *The Rule*

The questioning on Mary's part was a legitimate dialogue to determine God's will for her. Everyone seeking God's holy will for his or her own life needs to do the kind of personal and spiritual inventory Mary did. Suddenly launching into a venture, without proper spiritual reflection and dependence on the Holy Spirit, will spell disaster for any one of us.

A good and wise spiritual director, a good personal friend, or a loving and devoted parent can all help us answer the "how" question.

Connecting Our "Hows" With Mary's

In answering the "how" question at any time of our life, we could do no better than enlist the support of the Blessed Mother, especially through the great prayer of the Rosary.

When I celebrate an annual gathering with the Hispanic and Vietnamese communities in our diocese, Marian devotion is always a strong element of those liturgies. Both cultures bring strong ties of devotion to the Blessed Mother. The Hispanics from Mexico honor her especially as Our Lady of Guadalupe from the miraculous image left on St. Juan Diego's *tilma,* while the Vietnamese have a special devotion to Our Lady under the titles of Our Lady of LaVang or Our Lady of Vietnam.

The processions and the prayers of the Rosary that accompany them strengthen both immigrant cultures as they find in the Blessed Virgin a model for facing the "hows" that inevitably arise daily in the life of those starting over in a new land. We have much to learn from their devotion and faithfulness.

I suggest that praying the Rosary daily would be linking ourselves with Mary and seeking her intercession in knowing ourselves better and being able to better respond to the challenges Jesus gives us in life.

Like no other intercessor among the saints of God, Mary helps us ask the right questions of God. She also helps us be both practical about the realities we face in life and trusting in God's power to do the impossible in our lives. Mary helps us ask God how something is possible and, hearing the answer to our question, respond in deep faith and trust in God. "Let thy holy will be done, Lord. I am your loving and faithful servant, always!"

Dan, a seminarian studying for the Diocese of Charleston, faced a tragic illness that descended upon him quickly and ultimately took his life. Medical science held out no hope for him; his family, his brother seminarians, and I were devastated. When his pain became unbearable, his only relief came from pressing a button that released medication into his system. Watching this situation as I visited with him one day, I suggested to him that he grab onto his Rosary at those times for spiritual help. The Blessed Mother would bring spiritual "pain relief" to his incredible suffering.

Later on another visit, Dan told me that he had taken my advice and had experienced great spiritual support in the midst of his physical suffering. He felt that the Blessed Mother was there to help him through all his pain, as only a mother's presence can solace a suffering child.

Praying the Rosary three times daily is part of the regimen of the Our Lady of Hope Community in St. Augustine, Florida. By praying the Rosary, this community of people, all of whom have suffered various forms of addiction, have experienced liberation. They find strength, consolation, and support through a strong devotion to Our Blessed Mother.

How long, O LORD?
Will you forget me forever?
How long will you hide
your face from me?
How long must I bear pain
in my soul,
and have sorrow in my
heart all day long?
How long shall my enemy
be exalted over me?

— Ps. 13:1-2

The foundress of this community, Mother Elvira Petrozzi, helps people who are lost find their way to Jesus and His special way of life through the intercession and power of the Blessed Virgin Mary. Lives are changed, and hope is given to the hopeless, with the help of this great devotion, the Rosary of Our Lady.

Marian Shrines

In the summer of 2006, I visited the Sorrowful Mother Shrine in Bellevue, Ohio. The shrine commemorates the sorrows of Mary that were linked with the sufferings of her divine Son. In one of the prayers in a booklet published by the shrine are the words of a prayer to the Sorrowful Mother: "How often you have come to my aid in moments of trial and despair! How many times you have lighted my way when darkness surrounded me!"[9]

How often Mary has been a source of consolation, guidance, and hope in our lives when troubles weigh us down. In sorrow and in joy, Mary is there to guide and support us, to show us always the pathway to Jesus, her Son, and His holy will for us.

At another shrine, dedicated to Our Lady of Consolation in Carey, Ohio — not far from where I lived as a child — there is an interesting display in the basement of the Basilica Church. Here the pilgrim will find what pilgrims before him or her have left behind:

> crutches . . .
> stretcher . . .
> liquor bottles . . .
> cigarettes . . .
> other items depicting some physical ailment; others, spiritual.

These items and the stories behind them testify to the transforming power of believing — like the Blessed Virgin Mary, truly a Mother of Consolation for all her children — that with God, nothing is impossible. No matter what the "how" we are faced with at the present moment:

- How will I ever walk again?
- How will I ever stop drinking?
- How will I get my children to come back to the Faith?

How, how, how?

Indeed, "How can this be?" For human beings, some things may be impossible, but with God, all things are possible. Pray to Mary daily, and she will help you answer the question, "How, Lord?"

PRAYER

Mary, Mother of God and my mother,
I often ask God how I can take on the daily challenges
of life before me.
They seem to be so many, and at times, so great.
How could God expect me to be a good _____
(fill in this blank for yourself)?
I am so weak, so immature, so human, so sinful.

Pray for me, Blessed Mother, that I may respond
to God's invitation to love Him
and serve Him
and His people
the way you did, with deep and abiding faith
and with joyful trust.
Help me to answer the call of God to me as you did.
"Let thy holy will be done, Lord! I am your loving and
faithful servant, now and always!" Amen.

Additional Resources

For an excellent overview of the Rosary, read the Apostolic Letter of Pope John Paul II, "On the Most Holy Rosary"— *Rosarium Virginis Mariae*, October 16, 2002.

A good small book on the Rosary based on Pope John Paul's Apostolic Letter is *Praying the Rosary with the Joyful, Luminous, Sorrowful, & Glorious Mysteries* by Michael Dubruiel and Amy Welborn (Our Sunday Visitor Publishing Division, 2003 and 2005); and the longer *The Rosary: Chain of Hope* by Benedict J. Groeschel, C.F.R. (Ignatius Press, 2003).

A visit to any of the numerous shrines dedicated to the Blessed Mother in this country and abroad will also bring great spiritual comfort and support. At the Shrine of Our Lady of La Leche in St. Augustine, Florida, many an expectant mother facing a difficult delivery has found hope and strength; many childless husbands and wives, after praying at the shrine, have been blessed with children. See the books *Marian Shrines of the United States: A Pilgrim's Guide* by Theresa Santa Czarnopys and Thomas M. Santa, Ligouri Press, 1998; *Shrines of Our Lady: A Guide to Fifty of the World's Most Famous Shrines* by Peter Mullen, St. Martin's Press, 1999; and, for novenas used at shrines (including Our Lady of La Leche), *The Church's Most Powerful Novenas*, by Michael Dubruiel (Our Sunday Visitor Publishing Division, 2006).

III. When?

When, Lord?

*"Lord, when was it that
we saw you...?"*
— MT. 25:37

Here and Now!

Two major questions beginning with the word "when" occur toward the end of Matthew's Gospel. One deals with "when" the end time will occur and the coming of Jesus will take place (Mt. 24:3). The other arises in the description Jesus makes of the final judgment (Mt. 25:31-46), "when the Son of Man comes in His glory, and all the angels with Him," seated on His royal throne, with all the nations assembled before Him.

The Son of Man will separate them into two groups as a shepherd separates sheep from goats. Those inheriting the kingdom (the sheep), separated on the right, are the ones who recognized the Lord in the hungry and thirsty, the stranger and the naked, the sick and imprisoned; those not inheriting the kingdom (the goats), separated on the left, are the ones who did not recognize Jesus in those same people.

*My soul thirsts for God,
for the living God.
When shall I come and behold
the face of God?*

— PS. 42:2

And the question asked by both those on the right and those on the left is the same question: "Lord, when was it that we saw you . . . ?"

So do not be afraid; you are of more value than many sparrows.

— Mᴛ. 10:31

When Will the World End?

The first "when" question in chapter 24 of Matthew's Gospel finds a resolution of sorts in the answer to the "when" question of chapter 25.

In chapter 24, Jesus talks about signs of the end time and "early stages of the birth pangs" of that end time. But he clearly avoids indicating any exact time. "But about that day and hour no one knows, neither the angels of heaven, nor the Son, but only the Father" (Mt. 24:36).

After the End — the Judgment

Chapter 25 of Matthew's Gospel provides a moral inventory for the followers of Jesus to determine that he or she is prepared for that end time, with the Parable of the Ten Bridesmaids with their lamps going out to welcome the groom, five foolish and five wise; with the Parable of the Silver Pieces and how well the servants handled funds entrusted to them; and finally the Last Judgment scene, where the Son of Man comes in His glory to render judgment.

With participation in the Eucharist, Catholics should naturally take greater interest in the poor and suffering and try to build a more just society. Those who nourish themselves with the faith of Christ at the Eucharistic table assimilate his same style of life, which is the style of attentive service, especially to the weakest and most disadvantaged.

— Pᴏᴘᴇ Bᴇɴᴇᴅɪᴄᴛ XVI

And the focus of the judgment scene of Mt. 25:31-46 is on how we've acted in the "here and now" of this life to assist those most in need in our midst. In doing good for the needy in the here and now, we come to the rescue of Jesus Christ himself.

In Matthew's Gospel, Jesus is telling us not to focus so much on the "when" of the Lord's coming at the end time, but the "when" of the Lord's coming, day to day, in our midst.

If we recognize Jesus now in the hungry and thirsty, the stranger and the naked, the sick and the imprisoned, Jesus will recognize us on Judgment Day as the ones inheriting His kingdom. Our eternal happiness hinges on our moral and spiritual capacity to recognize Him and serve Him where He is in this world, in the time frame in which we are on earth.

Meeting the Lord

Blessed Teresa of Calcutta and the Missionaries of Charity, the community that she founded, are known worldwide for their aid to the poor and the outcasts of the world. They often are found where others will not go. What gives them the strength to minister in such harsh situations? The secret, Mother Teresa would tell an inquirer, was in how the community began its day — in prayer before Jesus present in the Most Blessed Sacrament. It was union with that Lord of the Eucharist that sustained her in her love of God and neighbor. Contemplating Jesus in the Holy Eucharist enabled her to see and serve Him in the thousands of needy people she met.

If we do not recognize Jesus in the poor, He will not be able to recognize us at the Day of Judgment.

— BL. TERESA OF CALCUTTA

Pope John Paul II in his encyclical on the Eucharist said that "to contemplate Christ involves being able to recognize Him wherever He manifests Himself, in His many forms of presence, but above all in the living sacrament of His body and blood."[10]

The Holy Father noted that not only does the Church draw its very life from Christ in the Eucharist as we are fed by the Lord, but it is also through the Eucharist that we are enlightened.[11]

We can conclude that through the Eucharist we are "enlightened" to discover Christ in those around us crying out for help. And the Eucharist gives us the wisdom and strength to go one step further — to give concrete and constructive help to those in need.

The answer to both of the "when" questions at the beginning of this chapter might be best stated as: when we discover the Lord of the Eucharist, we are able to put these "when" questions into the proper perspective.

It is the Lord of the Eucharist whose coming in the present overshadows the question of when the Lord will come at the end of time. Totally absorbed with the Lord's present coming in the Eucharist, we are not anxious about the timing of the Lord's future coming, at the end of time.

The Lord of the Eucharist helps us to be enlightened to recognize His presence in the people around us in our everyday lives who are in need of our help, care, and concern; and the Lord of the Eucharist gives us the wisdom and strength to address their needs in the most fitting ways possible.

We might want to avail ourselves of opportunities for Adoration of the Blessed Sacrament to allow the Holy Eucharist to nourish us, in the best ways, and give us strength to reach out and help those most in need in our midst. Could we support taking time out for intimate conversation with God — in this special, unique way — in the course of the day, to bring our prayer, "When, Lord?" to the God who awaits us?

I think of the hundreds of people who pray daily before the Lord in special adoration chapels consecrated for this purpose in churches throughout our diocese and throughout the world, some of them providing opportunities for Eucharistic Adoration twenty-four hours a day.

PRAYER

Like others, Lord,
I am sometimes anxious about the end time,
wanting to know, are we on the threshold
of Your return?
But help me to see when I might be staring
You in the face
as You come to me now in the people
I live with,
work with,
and see all around me.
Fill me with the desire to always
seek Your Face, Lord!
Move me more and more to adore You in
the Most Blessed Sacrament ,where You are truly present,
and to pray earnestly for Your coming!
Then open my eyes to see You under Your many guises
as You come to me throughout the day.
Amen.

Additional Resources

Pope Benedict XVI's encyclical *Deus Caritas Est,* 2006

Pope John Paul II's encyclical *Ecclesia de Eucharistia,* 2002

Cardinal Francis Arinze, *The Holy Eucharist* (Huntington, IN: Our Sunday Visitor, 2001)

The *Praying in the Presence of Our Lord* series of books edited by Father Benedict Groeschel (Huntington, IN: Our Sunday Visitor). This series includes books geared toward Eucharistic adoration and praying with such greats as Mother Teresa, Fulton Sheen, Dorothy Day, St. Thérèse, and St. Padre Pio.

Bishop Robert J. Baker and Father Benedict Groeschel, *When Did We See You, Lord?* (Huntington, IN: Our Sunday Visitor, 2005)

IV. What?

What, Lord?

*"Teacher, what good deed must I do
to have eternal life?"*
— MT. 19:16

The Purpose of Life

The question put by the man in Matthew's Gospel, described as young and as having many possessions (Mt. 19:22), was related to the moral and spiritual life. He was touching on the major issues discussed by moral theologians and ascetic theologians throughout the Christian era. "Teacher, what good deed must I do to have eternal life?" (Mt.19:16).

It was a question that we can translate into the issue of what particular vocation in life an individual is being called to: single or married life, religious life, the diaconate, or the priesthood. It is the question of discernment of one's vocation.

What Do I Need to Do?

In the case of the rich young man, Jesus pointed out that the bottom line for possessing everlasting life was keeping the commandments. Jesus cites several of the Ten Commandments, as well as the commandment from Lev. 19:18 to love one's neighbor as oneself.

*"And now, LORD,
what do I wait for?
My hope is in you."*

— PS. 39:7

Remember that Jesus explained to the Pharisees that the two greatest commandments of the law were to love the Lord with one's whole heart, soul, and mind (Deut. 6:5) and to love one's neighbor as oneself (Lev. 19:18) (cf. Mt. 22:36-40).

The rich young man says he has kept all the commandments Jesus mentioned. "What do I still lack?" (Mt. 19:20). Another "what" prayer, but this time he is moving beyond the level of simple morality to the level of a more intense spiritual life.

Jesus then tells the young man, if he is seeking perfection, to sell all of his possessions and give to the poor, then come back and follow Him (Mt. 19:21). That was the last time the rich young man asked the Lord any questions. It was the end of the spiritual dialogue. Matthew's Gospel says the young man went away sad, "for he had many possessions" (Mt. 19:22).

Material goods kept the rich young man from aspiring to perfection. And Jesus tells his disciples: "It will be hard for a rich person to enter the kingdom of heaven" (Mt. 19:23). It would not be impossible; just very difficult.

It would be easier for a "camel go through the eye of a needle than for someone who is rich to enter the kingdom of God" (Mt. 19:24). But Jesus also pointed out that "for mortals it is impossible, but for God all things are possible" (Mt. 19:26).

This was the point in Matthew's account where Peter interjected his concern and question: "Look, we have left everything and followed you. What then will we have?" (Mt. 19:27).

Jesus did not put off Peter's question. It was a sincere question. Unlike the rich young man, Peter and the other eleven had turned their backs on their past lives to follow Jesus. What was in store for the likes of them? Jesus tells them they will take their places on twelve thrones to judge the twelve tribes of Israel (Mt. 19:28).

"And everyone who has left houses or brothers or sisters or father or mother or fields, for my name's sake, will receive a hundredfold, and will inherit eternal life" (Mt. 19:29).

The answer to Peter is an answer that might be seen as an extended answer to the rich young man. Had the young man stuck around a little longer, he might have heard Jesus' more extensive commentary on how to gain everlasting life.

Our "What" Questions
We may be asking similar "what" questions of Jesus:

- What is God calling me to do with my life?
- What must I do to possess everlasting life?
- What "more" can I do?
- What rewards await a person who abandons all to follow Christ?

In asking these questions of God, it would be well to invoke the presence and guidance of the Holy Spirit in a special way, asking that the gifts we received from Him at our baptism and confirmation empower us not only to hear the answers to our "what" questions, but, like the apostles, to be moved to put them into action.

Invoking the Holy Spirit
The Holy Spirit is present in our lives to help us find our way to meaning, purpose, and direction in life. The Holy Spirit always enlightens us to the way of Jesus for us. The Holy Spirit helps us discern the will of the Lord for us, leading us to God our Father and to everlasting life.

In his book, *Lifework: Finding Your Purpose in Life,*[12] Rick Sarkisian highlights the fact that all human beings are "laborers in the vineyard; each of us [is] God's child using the gifts, talents, and abilities He has given to us. . . . Whether we are called to the priesthood, marriage, or consecrated life, we join together in service to God for the Church."[13]

Sarkisian suggests that discovering, accepting, and making a commitment to one's personal vocation involves entering into a lifelong process of listening for God's call. One acknowledges his or her God-given talents and abilities as gifts, then follows God's lead in accepting them in performing one's tasks in life.

Sarkisian does something many counselors of youth do not do in guiding their directees to discerning their gifts and vocation: he roots the discerning process in a relationship with God and a living out of the virtuous life. He writes:

> Remember the young man in the Gospels who asked Jesus, "What must I do to inherit eternal life?" Pope John Paul II teaches that he was asking, "What must I do that my life may have meaning? What is God's plan for my life? What is His will?" Jesus says, "Follow me." You, like the young man, are therefore called to follow Jesus.[14]

God calls you by name in a way that emphasizes your unique identity as His child. Sarkisian proposes that young people consider the influence of values, virtues, and faith on the career-making process. "Virtues are like a lighthouse that shines its beam through fog. It is a light to follow, even when life's journey is unclear, hazy, or difficult."[15] Sarkisian does not overlook the occupational elements in discerning one's vocation in life such as talents, skills, and interests, in addition to other occupational considerations. He simply links these values with the spiritual elements of values, virtues, beliefs, and spiritual gifts. "These spiritual elements are illuminated by the light of the Holy Spirit shining through the lens of prayer, Scripture, and Church teaching."[16]

The Sacrament that Makes Us God's Stewards

The Holy Spirit's role must be factored into any effort at helping young people discern God's will for them and their life's vocation and career.

I like to describe this as the "stewardship" dimension of life. The Sacrament of Confirmation enables the Holy Spirit to work in a tangible and powerful manner to help young people discern the gifts of time, talent, and treasure they have available to offer to become co-workers with Jesus Christ in building up His kingdom on earth.

The gifts and fruits of the Spirit bestowed on them in the Sacrament of Confirmation help them better understand what their gifts and talents are, and enable them to put these gifts and talents to work, rather than "hiding them under a bushel basket."

I suggest that catechetical programs and high school religion classes adopt a format to help young people discern their call in life, guided by the Holy Spirit. Too little is done to help this process along that was begun at baptism and furthered in the Sacrament of Confirmation, the sacrament of Christian stewardship.

We should make recourse to the Holy Spirit daily for wise decision-making in all aspects of life, but specifically vocational decisions. The Holy Spirit will guide those who seek His direction and support in living out the Christian life.

One of the great blessings I have as a bishop is to bring people being confirmed the Gifts of the Holy Spirit. Among the celebrations I have had of this great sacrament was a reception into the Church and confirmation of an inmate at one of our state prisons, Evans Correctional Institution, in Bennettsville, SC. Father. Francis Obong (while he was pastor of parishes in Cheraw and Bennettsville) had already prepared this candidate for the Sacrament of Confirmation and for the reception of two other sacraments as well, the Sacraments of Reconciliation and Holy Eucharist.

Divested of his earthly possessions through incarceration, this man was able to be led by the Holy Spirit to discern God's holy will for him and to respond generously and graciously to that invitation. He had a great deal of time on his hands to listen to the promptings of the Holy Spirit. A prison can become like a monastery, where the Holy Spirit is able to reach a person in a way that no one else has been able; as a result, many conversions can, and do, take place in prison cells.

I have met hundreds of other candidates and catechumens who are preparing to enter the Catholic Church at the Easter Vigil ceremony during the Rite of Election. These people asked similar questions to those the rich young man and Peter asked, and the Holy Spirit guided them to an answer.

Ask similar questions of Jesus yourself, then enlist the Holy Spirit's help in answering them. You may be surprised at the outcome: the Holy Spirit will lead you to answers beyond your wildest expectations.

PRAYER

What do You want of me, Lord?
What must I do to possess everlasting life?
What more can I do with my life?
What can I expect when I leave everything
to follow You?
Come, Holy Spirit, enlighten my heart,
enkindle within me the fire of Your love.
Strengthen my will to do good,
to do Your holy will in faith, hope, love, and joy.
Guide me to know what is right and to be eager
to do Your will for me.
Aided with Your power I will offer my time,
talent, and treasure to help You renew
the face of the earth.
Amen.

Additional Resources

Rick Sarkisian, Ph.D., *LifeWork: Finding Your Purpose in Life* (San Francisco, Ignatius Press, 1997)

Other resources by Dr. Sarkisian are:

The Video Companion to the Book *LifeWork*

A video, *Completely Christ's: The Radical Call to the Consecrated Life*

The LifeWork Journal: A Weekly Notebook for the Story of Your Life

LifeWork: A Workbook to Help You Find, Follow, & Fulfill Your Purpose in Life (with Leader's Guide and Curriculum Manual)

The Drive Factor: Getting Your Life in Gear for the 7 Areas That Matter Most

The Mission of the Catholic Family: On the Pathway to Heaven

and

The LifeWork Inventory: A Navigational Guide for the 7 Areas of Life That Matter Most.

Sarkisian invites parents to be vital partners in helping their children understand their talents and vocation in life. Quoting Pope John Paul II's 1994 *Letter to Families*, he reminds parents of the Holy Father's valuable message:

Parents are the first and most important educators of their own children, and they also possess a fundamental competence in this area — they are educators because they are parents . . . and . . . within the context of educator, due attention must be paid to the essential question of choosing a vocation and . . . in particular that of preparing for marriage.

Sarkisian suggests that, in order to promote wise and prayerful vocation choices, "parents must encourage their children to seek God's call." He provides videos and other guides as additional help to broaden the base of his great insights.

Other resources:

St. Ignatius, *The Spiritual Exercises of St. Ignatius* (available from various publishers)

Fishers of Men video on the priesthood, by the United States Conference of Catholic Bishops' Vocations Committee

A brochure on teenagers and stewardship (soon to be published in English and Spanish) by the United States Conference of Catholic Bishops, Albert L. Winseman, D. Min.

Donald O. Clifton, Ph.D. and Curt Liesveld, M. Div., *Living Your Strengths: Discover your God-given Talents and Inspire Your Community, Catholic Edition* (Gallup Press. New York, NY: 2003, 2006)

V. Where?

Where, Lord?

"Where are we to get enough bread in the desert to feed so great a crowd?"
— MT. 15:33

Where Can I . . . ?

Somewhere along the line, Moses — the great man of faith and leader of the Chosen People, who freed his people from bondage of Pharaoh and the Egyptians — stopped fully believing and trusting that God's promises would be fulfilled.

While tending the flock of his father-in-law, Jethro, the priest of Midian, Moses met the Lord, "the God of Abraham, the God of Isaac, the God of Jacob," in the burning bush at the mountain Horeb, and he "hid his face, for he was afraid to look at God" (Ex. 3:1-6).

From that special experience, Moses began a dialogue with God that involved many questions asked in faith:

"Who am I that I should go to Pharaoh, and lead the Israelites out of Egypt?"
— Ex. 3:11

"If I come to the Israelites and say to them, 'The God of your ancestors has sent me to you,' and they ask me, 'What is his name?' what shall I say to them?"
— Ex. 3:13

"O LORD, why have you mistreated this people? Why did you ever send me? Since I first came to Pharaoh to speak in your name, he has mistreated this people, and you have done nothing at all to deliver your people."

— Ex. 5:22-23

So Moses said to the LORD, "Why have you treated your servant so badly? Why have I not found favor in your sight, that you lay the burden of all this people on me? Did I give birth to them, that you should say to me, 'Carry them in your bosom, as a nurse carries a sucking child,' to the land that you promised on oath to their ancestors? Where am I to get meat to give to all this people? For they come weeping to me and say, 'Give us meat to eat!' I am not able to carry this people alone, for they are too heavy for me. If this is the way you are going to treat me, put me to death at once — if I have found favor in your sight — and do not let me see my misery."

— NUM. 11:11-15

The Lord accepted the questions and grumblings of the people of Israel, but only up to a point. Eventually, the Lord lowered the boom and rendered a verdict found in chapter 14 of the book of Numbers:

"How long shall this wicked congregation complain against me? I have heard the complaints of the Israelites . . . and of all your number, included in the census, from twenty years old and upward, who have complained against me, not one of you shall come into the land in which I swore to settle you, except Caleb son of Jephunneh and Joshua son of Nun."

— NUM. 14:26-30

A specific verdict is rendered on Moses and Aaron in chapter 20 of Numbers after Moses struck a rock twice with his staff, rather than just once, to bring water for his people, indicating a hesitancy of belief in God on his part:

> *"Because you did not trust in me, to show my holiness before the eyes of the Israelites, therefore you shall not bring this assembly into the land that I have given them."*
>
> — NUM. 20:12

God was very patient with the people of Israel in all their questionings. Once He had taught them about His providential love and His faithfulness to them, God would not tolerate a kind of questioning based on doubt of His presence and of His providence. Moses, Aaron, and the people of promise had stepped over the line of faith to disbelief. God would teach them a lesson. The adults were not to make it to the Promised Land.

In our life, too, questioning God is okay, if it is a question based on belief in Him and trust in His Divine providence.

"I Have Loved Jesus in the Night"

It may surprise some that a woman so obviously filled with faith as Blessed Teresa of Calcutta often prayed the Questioner's Prayer.

Bishop William Curlin, now the retired bishop of Charlotte, was a close friend of Blessed Teresa, visited her often, and on occasion gave retreats to her sisters. Once on a thirty-day retreat he was giving to the sisters in Calcutta before he was a bishop, he received a short note sent across the room to him by Mother Teresa. He unfolded the simple note and read it: "Father, please pray for me ... Where is Jesus?"

BlessedTeresa, in the last years of her life, experienced the mystical "dark night of the soul." This is a state of spiritual darkness where God's "presence" may be best described as His seeming "absence." In this state, one's prayer life feels dry; indeed, one's entire spiritual life is an intense experience of the desert. The faculties of the soul are brought to a state of utter darkness in the experience of the light of Christ's presence. Christ is there, but the human senses no longer perceive the blessings of the Lord as before. What one is experiencing is the Lord of the blessings rather than the blessings of the Lord.

My tears have been my food
day and night,
while men say to me continually,
"Where is your God?"

— Ps. 42:3

St. John of the Cross has written extensively on this special state of spiritual growth. His books, *The Ascent of Mount Carmel* and *The Dark Night of the Soul,* are classics in the history of spirituality which describe the passage to spiritual union with God that takes place in this journey through spiritual darkness.

Mother Teresa's words, "Father, please pray for me . . . Where is Jesus?", elicited a discussion with Bishop Curlin, in which she gave the Bishop a spiritual gem. How did she handle this dark night? She told him what the key to heaven was for her: "I have loved Jesus in the night."

Blessed Teresa of Calcutta has described the depth of darkness of her dark night during which she continued to love Jesus:

- "Within me everything is icy cold. . . . It is only blind faith that carries me through. . . ."
- "I am longing with painful longing to be all for God, to be holy in such a way that Jesus can live His life to the full in me. The more I want Him, the less I am wanted. I want to love Him as He has not been loved, and yet there

is that separation, that terrible emptiness, that feeling of absence of God. . . ."

- "I did not know that love could make me suffer so much. That was suffering of loss, that is of longing, of pain, human, but caused by the divine."
- "I have come to love the darkness, for I believe now that it is a part, a very, very small part of Jesus' darkness and pain on earth."
- ". . . Today really I feel a deep joy that Jesus can't go anymore through the agony but that he wants to go through it in me. . . ."
- "When you feel in your own heart with the suffering of Christ, remember, the Resurrection has to come; the joy of Easter has to dawn."

According to her community, Mother Teresa's dark night continued from 1949 until 1997, the year of her death. She wanted God so much she gave herself totally to Him and, in her love for Him, experienced His absence as only lovers do.

Our question, "Where is Jesus? Where is God?" may not reflect Blessed Teresa's depth of faith. What she teaches us is that people of faith can be feeling the absence of God and be sincerely led to ask in prayer, "Where are you, God?"

Our "Where" Questions

Depending on our plight at any particular time in life, our "where" question might take many forms. It may not be of the spiritual intensity of the "dark night of the soul," but it may seem to us to be of that quality of spiritual darkness, given the situation we find ourselves in at the time.

A few examples of situations that spur us to ask the question: "Where are you, God":

- A husband or wife announces out of the blue that he/she no longer has any love for the spouse and wants out of the marriage.
- A son or daughter is discovered using illegal drugs and is not in the least remorseful or repentant, having no desire to seek help.
- Without any special warning or previous illness, a spouse is diagnosed with advanced stages of cancer.
- A family member or friend dies suddenly or tragically.
- Monumental international tragedies on the level of a tsunami wipe out thousands, or a terrorist act has similar consequences.

"Where Are You, God?"

Sometimes, we simply can't change circumstances. There comes a point where we have done everything humanly possible and have to face our limitations. Like the apostles faced with the enormity of the crowd to be fed in the Gospels, we approach the Lord with both faith and a tinge of embarrassment when we ask, "Where?" It is the darkness that we all face in life, but in a mysterious way, it is the portal to true faith and trust in God.

In a sense, the "where" prayer embraces all the other prayers of the questioners, as it brings us face-to-face with the reality of both our limitations and evil in our world. It is the cross in all its starkness that we come to face. But this is where our Faith reaches its pinnacle.

Pope Benedict XVI, in a catechesis on the Book of Revelation, offered a unique insight into how the "lamb who was slain" holds the key to pointing the way when our hearts are troubled with apparent defeat. In commenting on the scroll that "no one was found worthy to open" and the weeping that it caused John (Rev. 5:4), the Holy Father says:

Perhaps John weeping at the mystery of a story so hidden expressed the disconcertment of the Asiatic Churches at the silence of God in the face of the persecutions to which they were exposed at the time. It is a disconcertment that could well reflect our own dismay at the grave difficulties, incomprehension and hostility which even today the Church suffers in many parts of the world.[17]

The Holy Father points out that in spite of this anguish that we face, the Book of Revelation gives us hope, because the sealed scroll — our inability to comprehend all the evil that befalls the innocent — can and has been opened:

It turns out that only the immolated Lamb could open the sealed book and reveal its contents, thus making sense of a story that is often so apparently absurd. Only the Lamb could take from the book the instructions and teachings that Christians need for life, to which His triumph over death is both an announcement and a guarantee of the victory which even the beleaguered Churches would doubtless obtain. All the strongly imaginative language that John employs is aimed at offering this comfort.[18]

Jesus' cross holds out our hope. Whatever form or intensity our "dark night" may take for us, I suggest doing what my brother and sister-in-law, both of whom struggled with cancer, have done: have a strong recourse to the sacraments of the Church — especially the Sacrifice of the Mass, that memorial of Our Lord's passion, death, and resurrection, what John refers to in the Book of Revelation as the "Wedding Feast of the Lamb."

There are the questions: Is it good to be alive? Is God good, and is he really there, and does he really help? We are not spared these dark nights. They are clearly necessary, so that we can learn through suffering, so that we can acquire freedom and maturity and above all else a capacity for sympathy with others. There is no final or rational answer, no formula of life in which we could explain these things. For in those instances when it gets under our skin and goes to the heart there are other factors in play that can't be explained by a universal formula but in the end can only be worked through by undergoing personal suffering.[19]

— POPE BENEDICT XVI

The sacraments are spiritually intense avenues for us to encounter the powerful healing presence of the Lord when we are hurting. The Sacrament of the Holy Eucharist is the high point of our sacramental relationship with the Lord; we prepare for it through other sacraments, such as Baptism, Confirmation, Reconciliation, and, in time of illness, the Sacrament of the Anointing of the Sick. The Lord gave us these human/divine encounters with Himself during our lives in this world to help us offset those tragedies that bring us to the point of asking, "Where are you, Lord?" He knew we needed a human touch that would bring us the divine embrace. The seven sacraments of the Church are those unique and special encounters, at appropriate times of our lives, which help us answer the question, "Where are you, Lord?"

Avail yourself of them often, before disaster hits and the question about God's presence/absence begins to form in your mind and heart.

He is with us, even though He seems so far away.

The seven sacraments, the sacramentals that surround them, and the devotions associated with them all provide a framework for helping us through the dark nights of our lives.

They will help us, as they helped my brother and sister-in-law and Blessed Teresa of Calcutta discover that the key to heaven is to have loved Jesus in the night.

Holy Mass points the way for us to find answers when we ask, "Where are you, Lord?" He is there waiting for us and there leading us beyond our "where" questions to a discovery of His abiding presence as Lord of Word and Sacrament. Holy Mass celebrated once a week is just a small portion of our time given to God in this greatest of prayers.

Many Catholics make the effort during Advent and Lent to attend Mass daily, and some Catholics arrange their work schedule to attend Mass daily all year 'round. They find that special grace makes the rest of their day flow with greater clarity and purpose, to help answer the Questioner's Prayer: "Where are you, Lord?"

PRAYER

Please help me, Lord,
in the darkness of the night,
to keep on loving You,
no matter what,
even when the only prayer I seem to be able to
utter is "Where are You, Jesus?"
Weekly, daily,
I will come to You
where I have discovered You before,
in holy Mass.
There You are hidden,
yet revealed.
You are humbled,
yet exalted.
You are darkness,
but You are also light.
You are sign and symbol,
yet saving reality and Divine Presence.
There I find You always present,
my Lord and my God!
Amen.

Additional Resources

Michael Dubruiel, *How to Get the Most Out of the Eucharist* (Huntington, IN: Our Sunday Visitor Publishing Division, 2005)

————, The *How-To Book of the Mass* (Huntington, IN: Our Sunday Visitor Publishing Division, 2007)

Scott Hahn, *The Lamb's Supper: The Mass as Heaven on Earth* (New York, NY: Doubleday, 1999)

For St. John of the Cross and St. Teresa of Ávila: Kieran Kavanaugh, O.C.D. and Otilio Rodriquez, O.C.D., translators, *The Collected Works of St. John of the Cross*, and *The Collected Works of St. Teresa of Ávila, Vol. 1 and Vol. 2* (Washington, D.C.: Institute of Carmelite Studies)

VI. Who?

Who, Lord?

"Who then can be saved?"
— MT. 19:25

Who Can Enter?

Psalm 15 contains a liturgical scrutiny that took place at the entrance to the temple court. An Israelite wanting to enter the sacred space had to ask the temple official what conduct was appropriate. "O LORD, who may abide in your tent? Who may dwell on your holy hill?"

The answer to that "who" question is given in the psalm.

> *Those who walk blamelessly,*
> *and do what is right,*
> *and speak the truth from their heart;*
> *who do not slander with their tongue,*
> *and do no evil to their friends,*
> *nor take up a reproach against their neighbors;*
> *in whose eyes the wicked are despised,*
> *but who honor those who fear the LORD;*
> *who stand by their oath even to their hurt;*
> *who do not lend money at interest,*
> *and do not take a bribe against the innocent.*
>
> *Those who do these things shall never be moved.*

Jesus was asked a similar question, not about "who" could enter the temple, but "who" will enter the heavenly kingdom (Mt. 19:25).

What was Jesus' response? He takes a child from the crowd to demonstrate dramatically that "unless you change and become like children, you will never enter the kingdom of heaven."

"Whoever becomes humble like this child is the greatest in the kingdom of heaven" (Mt. 18:1-4).

The password for entrance into the kingdom of heaven is humility. The proud have no access to the kingdom.

Salvation

"Then who can be saved?" (Mt. 19:25). The context of this question in Matthew's Gospel is the story of the rich young man who was told what to do to inherit eternal life (cf. the "what" question of a previous meditation). For him, the struggle was not with pride but with greed. He walked away sad from Jesus' invitation to sell all and follow him, "for he had many possessions" (Mt. 19:22).

So Jesus asked the twelve, "Do you also wish to go away?" Simon Peter answered him, "Lord, to whom can we go? You have the words of eternal life. We have come to believe and know that you are the Holy One of God."

— Jn. 6:67-69

After hearing Jesus explain how difficult it is for a rich person to enter the kingdom of heaven, the disciples were astonished and asked, "Then who can be saved?" (Mt. 19:25). Rightly, the disciples were seeing that just being a follower of Jesus would not cut the mustard. Just having the name "Christian" was not going to bring them eternal happiness. Jesus reminds them that, "For mortals it is impossible, but for God all things are possible" (Mt. 19:26).

The Kingdom of God

Matthew's Gospel is the Gospel of the kingdom. After the arrest of John the Baptist, Jesus began to tell people to reform their lives. "The kingdom of heaven has come near" (Mt. 4:17). After choosing the twelve apostles, Jesus tells them to go after the lost sheep of the house of Israel and proclaim the same message (Mt. 10:6-7).

Jesus compares the kingdom of God to a man who sowed good seed in his field (Mt.13:24), a mustard seed (Mt. 13:31), a buried treasure (Mt. 13:44), and a dragnet (Mt. 13:47). And every scribe who is knowledgeable about the kingdom of God is like "the head of a household who can bring from his storeroom both the new and the old" (Mt.13:52).

Jesus teaches that His kingdom belongs to the poor in spirit (Mt. 5:3), those persecuted for holiness' sake (Mt. 5:10), and whoever fulfills and teaches his commands (Mt. 5:19). Unless a person's holiness surpassed that of the scribes and Pharisees, one would not enter the kingdom of God (Mt. 5:20).

Matthew's Gospel also talks about the foundations of the Church (Mt. 16:18). Jesus goes on to found His Church on Peter. " . . . you are Peter (*petros*, "rock"), and on this rock I will build my church, and the gates of Hades will not prevail against it" (Mt. 16:18). To Peter is entrusted the "keys of the kingdom of heaven" (Mt. 16:19).

The Second Vatican Council (*Lumen Gentium*, 5) and the *Catechism of the Catholic Church* (541, 567) refer to the Church as the seed and beginning of the kingdom. The Church is pivotal in one's arriving at the kingdom, arriving at salvation, in that "all salvation comes from Christ the head through the Church which is his Body" (*Catechism of the Catholic Church*, 846).

The Council taught that the Church is necessary for salvation because the one Christ is the mediator and the way of salvation; and He is present to us in His body, which is the Church.

He himself explicitly asserted the necessity of faith and Baptism, and thereby affirmed at the same time the necessity of the Church which men enter through Baptism as through a

door. Hence they could not be saved who, knowing that the Catholic Church was founded as necessary by God through Christ, would refuse either to enter it or to remain in it.
— *Lumen Gentium,* 14

The fathers of the Council further specified that people who ... through no fault of their own, do not know the Gospel of Christ or His Church, but who nevertheless seek God with a sincere heart, and, moved by grace, try in their actions to do His will as they know it through the dictates of their conscience — those too may achieve eternal salvation.
— *Lumen Gentium,* 16;
Catechism of the Catholic Church, 847

The Church always remains our way of experiencing the kingdom of God in the present until the Lord comes at the end of time, when the fullness of the kingdom will be revealed. The Church is the way Jesus chose for us to arrive at our salvation.

Saved?

"Then who can be saved?" That question is answered today in the context of the Church. The Church, through its sacramental life and its Sacred Scripture and Tradition, as interpreted by the Magisterium, provides us the authentic way to experience Jesus Christ, who leads us in the Holy Spirit to God the Father. The Church is one, holy, catholic, and apostolic in nature. Salvation is a process experienced at Baptism and continued as one journeys on the path to holiness of life. Through sin, one can rupture the union with Christ brought about by the saving grace of Baptism; the Sacrament of Reconciliation provides the avenue to restore the graced union lost by serious sin.

Now is always the time to allow the grace of Christ to touch us through His Church. It is the time to remember what lengths

What then are we to say about these things? If God is for us, who is against us? He who did not withhold his own Son, but gave him up for all of us, will he not with him also give us everything else? Who will bring any charge against God's elect? It is God who justifies. Who is to condemn? Is it Christ Jesus, who died, yes, who was raised, who is at the right hand of God, who indeed intercedes for us. Who will separate us from the love of Christ? Will hardship, or distress, or persecution, or famine, or nakedness, or peril, or sword? . . . No, in all these things we are more than conquerors through him who loved us.

— ROM. 8:31-35, 37

God went to bring healing and peace to people separated from His love by Original Sin or by personal sin. It is a time for us to ask the kind of questions that relate to our own salvation, as we prepare to receive the sacramental grace in the Sacrament of Reconciliation or, if a new Catholic, in the Sacrament of Baptism.

> *Join with me in suffering for the gospel, relying on the power of God, who saved us and called us with a holy calling, not according to our works but according to His own purpose and grace. This grace was given to us in Christ Jesus before the ages began, but it has now been revealed through the appearing of our Savior Christ Jesus, who abolished death and brought life and immortality to light through the gospel.*
> — 2 TIM. 1:9-10

Who can be saved? I can be saved. The Church is the way Jesus set in motion to unite me with His kingdom, the kingdom of God, the kingdom of heaven, the kingdom of the saved.

PRAYER

Like Your disciples,
I sometimes have trouble finding my way
to Your kingdom.
It just seems so elusive and hard to experience concretely.
I know I am far from being holy.
You want me to be perfect as my
heavenly Father is perfect,
but I have trouble seeing myself as holy.
I have trouble seeing the people around me,
even the people in Church, even the people serving
at the altar as holy.
Who then can be saved?
Help me to see the Church You established on Peter
as the avenue to my holiness of life,
my salvation in Jesus Christ.
Help me to look beyond my own weaknesses
and that of the other people around me
so that I may discover
Your grace at work
whenever Your Church acts through its sacramental life
and its authentic leaders and teachers.
I want to be among the saved,
and I know where to find You present,
teaching, guiding, and sanctifying — in Your Church.
Amen.

Additional Resources

Bishop Robert J. Baker, S.T.D., *The Redemption Of Our Bodies: The Theology of the Body and Its Consequences for Ministry in the Diocese of Charleston* (Charleston, SC: The Catholic Miscellany, 2005)

Cardinal Avery Dulles, *The New World of Faith* (Huntington, IN: Our Sunday Visitor, 2000)

Cardinal Avery Dulles in *John Paul II and the New Evangelization: How You Can Bring the Good News to Others*, edited by Ralph Martin and Peter Williamson, (Cincinnati, OH: Servant Publications, 2006)

Archbishop J. Michael Miller, C.S.B., *The Shepherd and the Rock: Origins, Development, and Missions of the Papacy* (Huntington, IN: Our Sunday Visitor, 1994)

Joseph Cardinal Ratzinger, now Pope Benedict XVI / Vittorio Messori, *The Ratzinger Report: An Exclusive Interview on the State of the Church* (San Francisco, CA: Ignatius Press, 1986)

Catechism of the Catholic Church: Second Edition (Washington, DC: USCCB, 2003)

Compendium of the Catechism of the Catholic Church (Washington, DC: USCCB, 2006)

United States Catholic Catechism for Adults (Washington, DC: USCCB, 2006)

Professor Thomas E. Woods, Jr., *How the Catholic Church Built Western Civilization* (Washington, DC: Regnery Publishing, Inc., 2005)

Epilogue

Our Lord's Question

"Who do you say that I am?"

— Mt. 16:15

Believing Someone Can Answer Us

My preoccupation with questions has been with the questions people address to God, which might at times seem problematic to them. To some people, questioning God suggests a lack of faith; when they have questions for God, no matter what the problem or dilemma causing the question, they wonder if that means that they don't believe in God anymore.

These reflections attempt to point out just the contrary: it's *failing* to ask God a question when one is dealing with a difficulty in life that may reflect a lack of faith. Jesus makes it clear that "for everyone who asks, receives, and everyone who searches, finds, and for everyone who knocks, the door will be opened" (Lk. 11:10).

> *Is there anyone among you who, if your child asks for a fish, will give a snake instead of a fish? Or if the child asks for an egg, will give a scorpion? If you then, who are evil, know how to give good gifts to your children, how much more will the heavenly Father give the Holy Spirit to those who ask him!*
>
> — Lk. 11:11-13

And when the heavenly Father sends the Holy Spirit, the Spirit provides a way; the Spirit provides an answer.

An Ethiopian priest friend shared with me a wonderful saying from his country. Transliterated, the words sound like *Teyaki Awaki*, and mean "One who asks is intelligent." Eastern ways of teaching give prominence to the role of questioning. As you read through the Bible, see how often questions set the stage for a teaching.

So don't feel guilty about questions; don't be shy about asking God anything. Sincere questions get serious answers from an attentive God, who is our loving Father. Ask those questions in prayer!

As Jesus was leaving the world, He reminded His followers that they would be sad for awhile, but He would see them again.

> *And your hearts will rejoice, and no one will take your joy from you. On that day you will ask nothing of me. Very truly, I tell you, if you ask anything of the Father in my name, he will give it to you. Until now you have not asked for anything in my name. Ask and you will receive, that your joy may be complete.*
>
> — Jn. 16:22-24

When we ask questions of the Father, we should ask them in Jesus' name. We are assured of an answer. The Lord wants us to approach the throne of the Father in His name with confidence, that our joy may be full.

Expecting Questions

I would like to conclude these reflections by simply pointing out that, as we ask questions of the Lord in prayer, Jesus will be asking questions of us as well, as He asked many questions of His disciples. There are books that detail the questions Jesus puts to His disciples, such as Msgr. Richard C. Antall's *Jesus Has a Question for You*, published by Our Sunday Visitor Press, 2002. You might look into the meditations in this and other books for a fuller treatment of the questions Jesus asks of His followers.

One of the questions that Jesus put to His disciples is especially worthy of our meditation: "Who do you say that I am?" (Mt. 16:15).

Jesus had previously asked His disciples, "Who do people say that the Son of Man is?" (Mt. 16:13). They were in the neighborhood of Caesarea Philippi when He chose to put these questions to His followers.

He went from a general question about others' theories and opinions, and the opinions of the "theologians," to confronting His disciples about their own personal convictions.

"Who do you say that I am?"

"You are the Messiah, the Son of the living God!" Simon Peter said in reply.

There was no hesitation, no wavering. Peter was firm in his response. He had, like the other apostles, asked Jesus many questions. Now it was test time for Peter. Now it was the Lord asking Peter directly, *What have you learned from your questions, Peter? After all your days with me, what conclusions have you personally come to? How well have I taught you in the classroom of life? How well have you paid attention? I always welcomed your questions. Now, how do you welcome mine?*

"Who do you say that I am?"

Jesus proceeds to acknowledge the depth of Peter's faith. *Petros* means "rock." On this rock, Jesus would build His Church, and the jaws of death would not prevail against it (Mt. 16:18). The good questioner ends up being the best learner, the faithful disciple, the leader and teacher of the faith — and all his successors after him, including our present pope, Pope Benedict XVI.

Our faith in Jesus is theirs. Our faith in Jesus is shored up by their faith. Ultimately though we must, each one of us, individually respond to that faith question of Mt. 16:15. All that we do as members of the Church is tied to our own personal response to that question. No one can answer the question for us. We answered it at our baptism, or, if we were too young then, at our reception of the Sacrament of Confirmation. Answer that question all of us must, sooner or later. It is the question of faith, personal faith in the Lord Jesus Christ.

The most important effort we can make as members of the Church is to help people discover Jesus in personal and communal prayer, so they can answer the question: "Who do you say that I am?" Jesus must be the central focus of everything we do in our Church. It is His mission and ministry that our Church exists to foster, His message that our Church exists to communicate, His ministry that our Church seeks to extend into the world.

The person and message of Jesus is the central thread interwoven throughout the life and activities of our Church, and His values are the ultimate norm and criterion by which all our decisions are made and against which all the results are evaluated. It is principally in the Holy Eucharist that we find Him revealed and present, Body and Blood, Soul and Divinity. In that sacrament we are best able to answer the question He puts to us, "Who do you say that I am?" As we encounter the Lord of the Eucharist, we are led, like Thomas, who personally examined the wounds of Jesus, to exclaim, "My Lord and my God!" (Jn. 20:28).

Our personal belief in Jesus as our Lord and God also sets the stage for our saying "yes" to Him in all the challenges He puts to us in life, easy and difficult. Conviction moves to commitment. The "yes" of belief yields to the "yes" of service, as did Mary's "yes" to the Archangel Gabriel, her "fiat."

An interesting meditation card that I carry in my Breviary reminds me, "Faith is not believing that God can. It is knowing that He will." That is the message of this book.

The Questioner's Prayer is a prayer of faith when the one praying that prayer knows from his or her past experience that God *will* intervene in one's life. That is the difference between the Questioner's Prayer of Mary and Zechariah. Mary knew from experience, from a profound life of faith, that God would come through in her life and do the impossible. Her prayer to God through the Archangel Gabriel was not an attempt to deny God's fidelity to her, but simply to ask how God would intervene to do the impossible in this humble maiden's life, so that she could, in turn, say "*Fiat*" — "Thy will be done!"

I'm reminded of the story my priest friend and mentor, a former abbot, told me about his struggle after entering a Trappist monastery. He had been a scholar and writer before, but was now facing some very mundane tasks; he'd been asked to put some curtains on a window, for example, and had no idea how to go about it. The switch from an active life of academia as a priest to living in a monastery was a major hurdle in life for him. So he went to a seasoned brother Trappist for advice on how to acclimate to this new and challenging way of life.

The old Trappist monk offered him some very simple yet profound advice: "Just say 'Yes, Jesus.'"

My friend did so, and not surprisingly, all has gone well for him in the monastic way of life ever since. In fact, he himself eventually become abbot of the monastery!

The answers to the questions we put to the Lord and the ones He puts to us are best resolved when we can say "yes" to the Lord from the depths of our hearts. He who put the question in our heart in the first place, He who asks us, "Who do you say I that profound response of faith, "Yes, Jesus," to Him in every event of life.

As we work through all our faith questions in life and listen to all the questions Jesus addresses to us through His Church, may His Holy Spirit help us find resolution in them through that prayer uttered at times personally, at times communally, but at all times fervently, the prayer of optimism and hope, born of an ever-deepened faith in God, Father, Son, and Holy Spirit: "Yes, Jesus, I embrace Your holy will for me always; I embrace You as my Lord and my God!"

Let that be the truest and most sincere of answers to all of our Questioner's Prayers!

Nothing can make man laugh unless there is an answer to the question of death. And conversely, if there is an answer to death, it will make genuine joy possible — and joy is the basis for every feast. At its heart, the Eucharist is the answer to the question of death.

— POPE BENEDICT XVI[20]

A Final Prayer

"Consummatum Est"

With outstretched hands,
I beg of Thee,
Father, hear my plea;
This cross has torn my body,
Be not far from me.

Grief and anguish plague me,
Wounds and pain are mine;
My blood-drenched eyes implore Thee,
Pity what is Thine.

They spit upon me, Father
They laugh, they scoff,
They chide.
In thy mercy hear me,
Hasten to my side.

Gone are health
and comfort.
Fled, as traitors flee.
The cross was made
for pain and death,
Not prosperity.

Sharp are the thorns
and nails,
Innocence cannot deceive.
Thou who knowest mercy,
Let this chalice take
its leave.

Yet Thy will is mine,
For Father, we are one.
What hath pleased the Father
Hath also pleased the Son.

Guiltless, forsaken, as a criminal,
I'm forced to die;
Forgive them for it, Father
And take the blame will I.

My head now seeks my bosom,
All strength and life depart.
Only love remains within me,
That and a severed heart.

To Thee I give my soul,
It hath now found rest.
For heaven is open and mankind saved.
Consummatum Est.

Acknowledgements

I am grateful to all who helped me in developing the meditations of *The Questioner's Prayer*. My first refection on this topic was an article in the *Florida Times-Union* in 1985, entitled "Jesus' Lessons Resulted Because He Was Questioned." I was encouraged in this effort by a staff writer for the Jacksonville, Florida, newspaper, Margo Pope, who has been associated with the *St. Augustine Record* in recent years.

Subsequently, Michael Dubruiel, Acquisitions Editor for Our Sunday Visitor Publishing Division, encouraged me to write on this topic in articles that appeared in our diocesan paper, *The Catholic Miscellany*. I am grateful to the editorial staff of *The Catholic Miscellany*, the first Catholic newspaper to be published in the United States.

I am also grateful to Our Sunday Visitor Publishing for its help in bringing this expanded version to fruition, as well as the work done on a previous book that centers on one question put to God in the Bible, *When Did We See You, Lord?* This question from the Last Judgment scene, found in Matthew's Gospel (25:31-46), was reflected on by Father Benedict Groeschel and myself in a series of meditations.

Kay Phillip, my Executive Assistant and typist, was a tremendous help in making the final text available for the publisher.

Chris Pelicano provided the artwork to enhance the message of this book's meditations.

To all of them —
and to all people of faith who pray the Questioner's Prayer, I say:

Thank you, and God bless you!

Notes

[1] *Salvifici Doloris,* Pope John Paul II, February 11, 1984.

[2] Charleston *Post and Courier,* May 6, 2006.

[3] Address of the Holy Father, Visit to the Auschwitz Camp, Auschwitz-Birkenau, May 28, 2006.

[4] The Charleston *Post and Courier.*

[5] The *Catholic Miscellany.*

[6] Published by Our Sunday Visitor, Inc. 2002.

[7] April 2, 2005; in the Church's liturgical calendar, the feast had already begun with the recitation of Evening Prayer I.

[8] *Salvifici Doloris,* Pope John Paul II, February 11, 1984 (paragraph 26).

[9] Rev. Anthony Telolis, C.PP.S., ed. *Sorrowful Mother Shrine Daily Prayers,* (Bellevue, OH: Sorrowful Mother Shrine), p. 25.

[10] *Ecclesia de Eucharistia* (6).

[11] Ibid. (6).

[12] (San Francisco, CA: Ignatius Press, 1997).

[13] *Lifework: Finding Your Purpose in Life* (San Francisco: Ignatius Press, 1997), p. 27.

[14] Ibid. p. 17.

[15] Ibid. p. 49.

[16] Ibid. p. 59.

[17] General Audience, Pope Benedict XVI, August 23, 2006.

[18] Ibid.

[19] *God and the World, A Conversation with Peter Seewald* (San Francisco, CA: Ignatius Press, 2002).

[20] *Benedictus: Day by Day with Pope Benedict XVI,* edited by Rev. Peter John Cameron, O.P. (Yonkers, NY: Magnificat/Ignatius Press, 2006).